STUDENT GUIDE

NUMBER POWERHOUSE

OPERATING WITH FRACTIONS, DECIMALS, AND PERCENTS

MathScape
SEEING AND THINKING MATHEMATICALLY

How can you use your own number sense to solve problems involving integers, fractions, decimals, and percents?

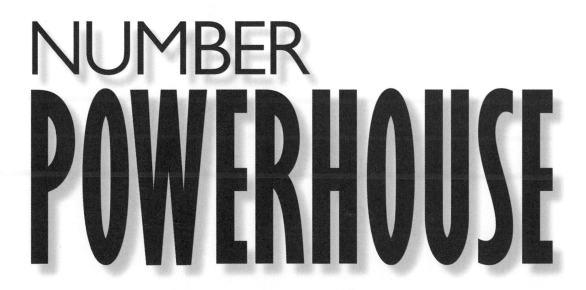

NUMBER
POWERHOUSE

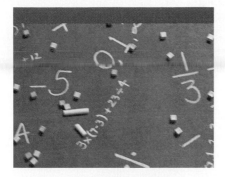

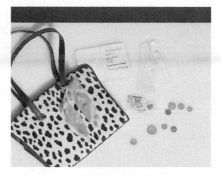

PHASE**ONE**
Integer Power

Your estimation skills and your ability to find the exact answers—using mental math, paper and pencil, or a calculator—are important in becoming a number powerhouse. In this phase, you will develop these skills with whole-number operations and use cubes to investigate rules for signed-number addition and subtraction.

PHASE**TWO**
Fraction Power

Many different strategies can be used to add, subtract, multiply, and divide fractions and mixed numbers. Solving these problems with paper and pencil using the rules you may have learned is one strategy. Other strategies are mental math and estimation, which you will explore in depth in this phase.

PHASE**THREE**
Decimal and Percent Power

In this phase, you will investigate decimals and percents. To help you figure out just where to place the decimal point when adding, subtracting, multiplying, and dividing decimals, you will use estimation and mental math. By using what you know about 50%, 10%, and 1%, you will be able to calculate the percents of any number.

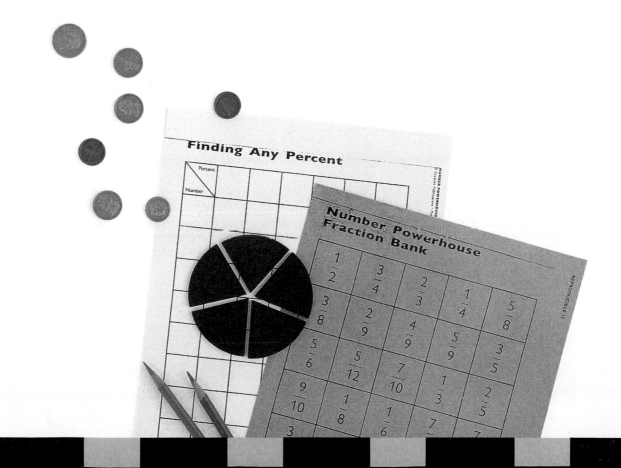

PHASE ONE

The mathematics that people need to use in everyday situations sometimes can be done with pencil and paper. But is that always the only and best way to go about adding, subtracting, multiplying, or dividing?

Estimation, mental arithmetic, and the calculator are also important tools for solving everyday problems. The most powerful method is the one that is most efficient and effective for the problem situation.

Integer Power

WHAT'S THE MATH?

Investigations in this section focus on:

COMPUTATION

- Understanding whole numbers and integers

- Adding, subtracting, multiplying, and dividing whole numbers

- Adding and subtracting integers

- Using paper and pencil, calculator, and mental math to get exact answers with whole numbers and integers

ESTIMATION

- Using estimation to check whether or not results are reasonable

- Understanding why an order of operations is necessary

Start with What You Know

You have known how to add, subtract, multiply, and divide whole numbers for a long time. But what do you *really* know about these operations? Here you will explore some useful ways to estimate and calculate answers to whole-number problems.

Play the "What MUST Be True?" Game

How much can you find out about an answer without doing calculations?

Sometimes it is more important to be able to give a quick estimate for an answer than to find the exact result. Try out your estimation skills as you play the "What MUST Be True?" Game.

1 Work with your group to write four problems that are difficult to solve quickly. Each problem should use a different operation: addition, subtraction, multiplication, or division. For each problem, write the following:

  a. three statements that you know MUST be true about the answer to this problem

  b. one statement about the answer that you know MUST be false

Scramble the true and false statements for a problem, so that the false one isn't always last. This will make your classmates work harder to find your false statement.

2 Exchange your group's problems and statements with another group. Figure out which statements for each problem MUST be true and which one MUST be false.

$477 \times 13 = ?$

I know that 477×13 is greater than 4000.

Use Different Methods to Solve Problems

Sometimes you need to know the exact answer to an arithmetic problem. However, there is more than one way to find a sum (or difference, product, or quotient)!

Calculate the answer to each problem in two different ways. Make notes about your two ways. If you use mental math to solve any of the problems without using pencil and paper, write down the thinking you used.

Problem 1	**Problem 2**	**Problem 3**	**Problem 4**
$6{,}413 + 9{,}892$	$12{,}348 - 4{,}837$	$147 \div 22$	713×19

Why do different methods produce the same answer?

What are some different ways to calculate answers to arithmetic problems?

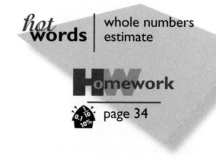

Write About Estimation and Exact Answers

Write your own problems that can be solved by adding, subtracting, multiplying, or dividing.

- Write one problem for which it makes sense to estimate a solution.

- Write another problem for which it makes more sense to find an exact answer.

Solve each problem and describe how you found your answer.

hot **words** | whole numbers
estimate

Homework

 page 34

2 Follow the Laws of Order

Order matters when you're putting on your shoes and socks, baking a cake, or setting a VCR to record your favorite program. You will see how the order in which you do addition, subtraction, multiplication, and division also makes a difference.

How does the order in which you perform operations affect the answer?

Evaluate an Expression in Different Ways

In the steps below, you will investigate different ways of evaluating the same expression. After you complete step 2, stop and participate in a class discussion before going on to step 3.

1 Use your calculator to evaluate the following expression: $14 \div 2 - 4 + 1 \times 6 \div 3 \times 2 + 10$. Enter the numbers and operation symbols from left to right. Press the $\boxed{=}$ key only after you enter the entire expression. Record your answer.

2 Try to figure out in what order the calculator evaluated the expression in step 1. Describe what you think is actually going on "inside" the calculator. Hint: One way to discover the order of operations a calculator uses is to record the number your calculator shows each time you press an operation sign.

3 Evaluate the expression in step 1 in a way that is different from the way you think your calculator did it. Explain your answer.

4 Exchange papers with a partner.

   a. Try to figure out what was going on inside your partner's calculator.

   b. Try to figure out how your partner evaluated the expression in a different way.

   c. Do you agree with the two ways your partner evaluated the expression? Why?

Use the Order of Operations

How can you use the order of operations to evaluate expressions?

What's the answer to a problem, such as $5 + 2 \times 3$, that has no parentheses to tell you which operation to do first? If you add first, then the answer you get is 21. If you multiply first, then the answer is 11. Mathematicians have developed a set of rules so that everyone will get the same answer. These rules are shown in the box below.

1 Use the order of operations to evaluate the expression shown below. Then use parentheses to get as many different answers as possible for the expression.

$$22 + 8 \div 4 - 3 \times 7$$

2 Write as many expressions as you can, using more than one operation that give each of the following answers:

a. 18 **b.** 50 **c.** 36

The Order of Operations

1. Evaluate expressions in parentheses.

2. Evaluate powers.

3. Do multiplication and division from left to right.

4. Do addition and subtraction from left to right.

For example, you would evaluate $32 - (5 + 3) \times 5 \div 2^2$ as follows:

$32 - (5 + 3) \times 5 \div 2^2$	Evaluate the expression in parentheses.
$32 - 8 \times 5 \div 2^2$	Evaluate the power.
$32 - 8 \times 5 \div 4$	Do the multiplication before the division, since it is further to the left.
$32 - 40 \div 4$	Do division before addition or subtraction.
$32 - 10$	
22	

hot **words** | order of operations
powers

Homework

page 35

Know How to Read the Signs

ADDING AND SUBTRACTING INTEGERS

You know how to add and subtract positive numbers. But what happens when negative numbers are mixed in? Here you will try showing numbers with "positive" and "negative" cubes to think about these problems.

Find Rules for Adding Integers

How can you develop rules for adding positive and negative numbers?

The handout Using Cubes to Add and Subtract Integers shows how you can use cubes to model adding with integers.

1 Write two example problems for each of these possible combinations:

a. Positive + Positive   **b.** Positive + Negative

c. Negative + Positive   **d.** Negative + Negative

2 Use cubes to experiment with the eight problems you have written. For each problem, sketch the cubes and write the equation.

3 Think about the equations you wrote and sketched. Write a set of rules that someone could follow when adding positive and negative numbers. Be sure your rules work for all problems with positive and negative numbers.

What Are Integers?

Integers are whole numbers (0, 1, 2, 3, 4, 5, ...) and their opposites. We call the whole numbers positive integers. We call their opposites negative integers. Zero is not positive and it is not negative. The figure below shows how integers appear on the number line.

$$\xleftarrow{\qquad} \begin{array}{ccccccccc} -6 & -5 & -4 & -3 & -2 & -1 & 0 & 1 & 2 \end{array} \xrightarrow{\qquad}$$

Find Rules for Subtracting Integers

You have found some rules for adding positive and negative numbers. Now you will create a set of rules for subtracting integers. The handout Using Cubes to Add and Subtract Integers shows how you can use cubes to model subtracting with integers.

1 List all of the possible combinations to subtract positive and negative numbers.

2 Experiment with cubes until you can write a rule for each possible combination. Be sure each rule tells how to find both the number and the sign of the answer.

3 Choose one especially tricky problem. Sketch the cubes and write about your solution.

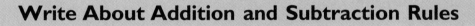

This is 4   minus -3.

There is +7 left!

How can you develop rules for subtracting positive and negative numbers?

Write About Addition and Subtraction Rules

Summarize the rules for adding and subtracting signed numbers. Make sure you include the following:

- Write the rules in your own words.

- Be sure you give rules for all positive and negative numbers.

hot **words** | positive integers
negative integers

Homework
page 36

4 The Problems Are All Yours

Some game shows give you an answer and ask you to provide the question. But does every answer have just *one* question? You will be given some "answers," and you will write as many addition and subtraction equations as you can for each of them. Then you will write a test about everything you have learned in this unit so far.

Represent Integers in Different Ways

If you are given an answer, can you write integer addition and subtraction equations with that result?

Here are some equations for which the answer is positive 4:

$2 + 2 = 4$, and $6 - 2 = 4$, and $-6 + 10 = 4$

Can you come up with a list of equations for which the answer is positive 4?

1 First make a list of addition equations whose answer is positive 4. Then make a list of subtraction equations whose answer is positive 4.

  a. Use cubes to help you get started.

  b. Look for patterns that can help you write more equations.

$$3 + 1 = 4$$

$$-1 + 5 = 4$$

2 Make a list of addition equations and a list of subtraction equations for each of these answers.

  a. −5   **b.** 0   **c.** 13   **d.** −12

Write a Test About Operations

Here's your chance—now, *you* get to write a test! Your test shouldn't be so easy that everyone gets all the answers right away, but it shouldn't be so hard that no one can do it.

There are six types of problems that should be on your test. Include at least one of each of the following problems:

1 An integer addition problem.

2 An integer subtraction problem.

3 A problem that involves addition, subtraction, multiplication, or division of whole numbers. In this problem, ask for the exact answer. Don't make the numbers too easy! There should be at least two digits.

4 A true/false problem about a sum, difference, product, or quotient of whole numbers. This problem should involve estimation skills, so be sure the numbers have at least two digits.

5 A problem that uses the order of operations rules. It should involve parentheses, powers, addition, subtraction, multiplication, and division. This must be a multiple-choice problem with at least four answer choices.

6 A writing problem that asks students to tell about something they have learned.

Prepare an answer key for your test. This will help you make sure your test isn't too easy or too difficult!

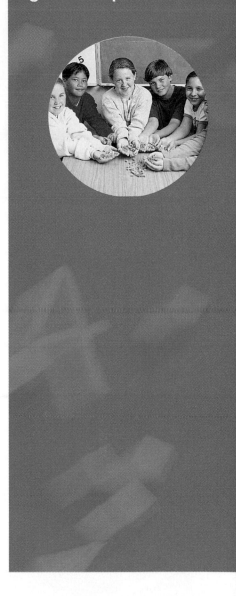

How can you write good test questions?

hot **words** | whole numbers integers

Homework page 37

PHASE TWO

In this phase you will be exploring fractions and mixed numbers. You will develop your own "number powerhouse" strategies by using estimation and mental math to help make sense of adding, subtracting, multiplying, and dividing fractions and mixed numbers.

Tools such as Fraction Circles and sketches can help you think about fraction operations. Why do you think they might be useful?

Fraction Power

WHAT'S THE MATH?

Investigations in this section focus on:

COMPUTATION

- Understanding fractions and mixed numbers

- Adding, subtracting, multiplying, and dividing fractions and mixed numbers

- Using paper and pencil, calculator, and mental math to get exact answers with fractions and mixed numbers

ESTIMATION

- Using estimation to check whether or not the results make sense

5 Pluses and Minuses

**ADDING AND
SUBTRACTING
FRACTIONS**

Quick—what's $\frac{3}{8} + \frac{5}{12}$? Although you may have learned rules for adding and subtracting fractions, those rules can be hard to remember or use quickly. Do you think you could solve this problem mentally? In this lesson, you will use what makes sense to you to develop your own number powerhouse strategies.

Use Thinking Strategies to Add Fractions

How can you solve fraction addition problems by using logical thinking?

You should have a set of fractions the class has chosen from the handout Number Powerhouse Fraction Bank. Follow the steps below to create fraction addition problems and find strategies that make sense to you for solving the problems. Remember, there is not just one "right way" to solve problems like these.

1 From the set of fractions your class agreed on, choose pairs of fractions to write fraction addition problems with. Try to challenge yourself by writing some addition problems that you think might be hard to solve.

2 Set aside any rules you might have learned and look for other ways to think about these problems that make sense to you. Use what you know about fractions.

3 Record your thinking for each problem. You may want to draw sketches to explain your thinking. The Fraction Circles are available to use. You will need to be prepared to give a Powerhouse Presentation to your classmates about your way of solving these problems.

Use Thinking Strategies to Subtract Fractions

Now that you have had some experience with new ways of thinking about addition problems, see what you can come up with for subtraction.

Can you solve fraction subtraction problems by using logical thinking?

1 From the set of fractions your class agreed on, choose pairs of fractions to write fraction subtraction problems with. What you know about comparing fractions will be important. The problems you write should involve subtracting a lesser fraction from a greater fraction.

2 Once again, set aside any rules you might have learned. Look for other ways to think about these problems that make sense to you and make it easier to solve the problems mentally.

3 Record your thinking for each problem. You may want to draw sketches to explain your thinking. The Fraction Circles are available to use. You will need to be prepared to give your classmates a Powerhouse Presentation on your way of solving these problems.

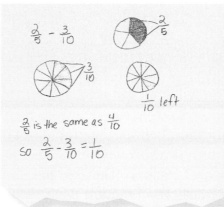

Write About Fraction Addition and Subtraction

Write about the strategies you used to add and subtract fractions mentally.

- Include an example of an addition problem and a subtraction problem you can solve mentally. Tell how you solved it.

- If you had different methods for different types of problems, explain how you decided which method to use.

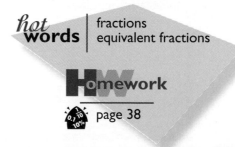

hot **words** | fractions
equivalent fractions

Homework
page 38

6 Multiplication Made Easy

MULTIPLYING FRACTIONS

If you understand the question behind a fraction problem, you can figure out the exact answer or make a mental estimate. With fraction multiplication, the key is thinking about groups. In this lesson, you will use this kind of thinking to get exact answers to easy fraction multiplication problems and estimates for more difficult ones.

Multiply Fractions by Thinking About the Question

How can you use what you know about the question asked by a fraction multiplication problem to solve the problem?

You will look for exact answers to fraction multiplication problems that can be solved mentally by just thinking about the question behind the problem. The secret is to read the multiplication symbol as "groups of." Follow these steps for each pair of fractions the class has chosen from the handout Number Powerhouse Fraction Bank.

1 Write out the question asked by the multiplication problem. The examples in the box What's the Multiplication Question? can help you think about the question.

2 Use the question to find the exact answer to the problem mentally. You may find it helpful to use Fraction Circles or sketches to help with your thinking.

3 Use sketches and words to explain your thinking. Be prepared to share your results and your thinking with the class.

What's the Multiplication Question?

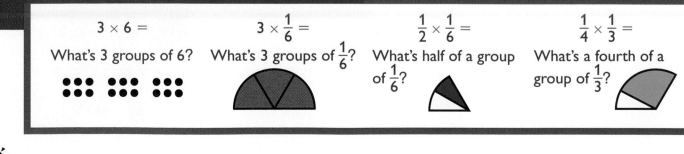

$3 \times 6 =$

What's 3 groups of 6?

$3 \times \frac{1}{6} =$

What's 3 groups of $\frac{1}{6}$?

$\frac{1}{2} \times \frac{1}{6} =$

What's half of a group of $\frac{1}{6}$?

$\frac{1}{4} \times \frac{1}{3} =$

What's a fourth of a group of $\frac{1}{3}$?

Estimate Answers to Multiplication Problems

For problems like $\frac{3}{4} \times \frac{7}{15}$ it would be difficult to find an exact answer mentally. But you can come up with an estimate by thinking about what you know for sure.

1 Choose pairs of fractions from the handout Number Powerhouse Fraction Bank.

2 For each pair of fractions, write a multiplication problem and list the things you know for sure.

3 Estimate the answer to the problem.

> What can you say for sure?
>
> Here are some "for sure" statements I can make about 3/4 × 7/15:
>
> · It asks the question "What's 3/4 of a group of 7/15?"
>
> · It's less than 7/15.
>
> · Half of 7/15 would be 3 and a half fifteenths, so it's more than that.

How can you estimate answers to problems that are not easy to solve mentally?

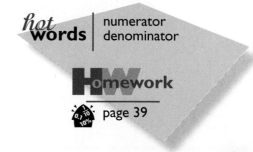

Write About How Estimates Compare to Exact Answers

For each fraction problem you answered with an estimation, calculate the exact answer by following the rules for multiplying fractions that you reviewed in class discussion. Write about how the estimate and the exact answer compare.

- How do the "for sure" statements you made compare to the exact answer?

- Can you think of situations in which it is useful to be able to estimate the answer to a fraction multiplication problem?

- When is it useful to be able to calculate an exact answer?

hot **words** | numerator denominator

Homework
page 39

The Great Fraction Divide

DIVIDING FRACTIONS

As with fraction multiplication, some problems that involve dividing fractions are easy to solve if you understand the question being asked. When you are a "number powerhouse," you can do more than just solve the problems. You can also explain what the answer means!

Divide Fractions by Thinking About the Question

How can you use what you know about multiplication to solve fraction division problems mentally?

In this investigation, you will look for exact answers to fraction division problems that can be solved mentally by just thinking about the question behind the problem. Follow these steps for each pair of fractions the class has chosen to work with from the handout Number Powerhouse Fraction Bank.

1 Write the question being asked by the division problem. The example in the box below can help you think about the question.

2 Use the question to find the exact answer to the problem mentally. You may find it helpful to use Fraction Circles or sketches to help with your thinking.

3 Use sketches and words to explain your thinking. Be prepared to share your results and your thinking with the class.

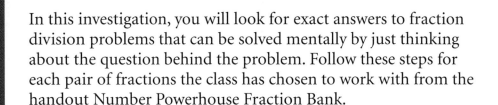

What's the Division Question?

$\frac{1}{6} \div \frac{1}{2}$

How many halves are there in $\frac{1}{6}$?

There is one-third of $\frac{1}{2}$ in $\frac{1}{6}$.

Estimate Answers to Fraction Division Problems

For problems like $\frac{3}{4} \div \frac{1}{7}$, it can be difficult to find an exact answer mentally. But you can come up with an estimate by thinking about what you know for sure.

1 Choose pairs of fractions from the Number Powerhouse Fraction Bank.

2 For each pair of fractions, write a division problem and list the things you know for sure.

3 Estimate the answer to the problem.

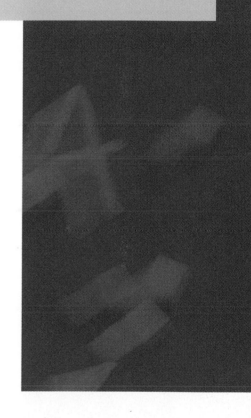

How can you estimate answers to fraction division problems that are not easy to solve mentally?

Write About Estimates and Exact Answers

For each fraction problem you answered with an estimation, calculate the exact answer by following the rules for dividing fractions that you reviewed in class discussion. Write about how the estimate and the exact answer compare.

- How do the "for sure" statements you made compare to the exact answer?

- Can you think of situations in which it is useful to be able to estimate the answer to a fraction division problem?

- When is it useful to be able to calculate an exact answer?

$\frac{3}{4} \div \frac{1}{7}$

How many $\frac{1}{7}$ ths are there in $\frac{3}{4}$?

· There are less than 7, because there are 7 sevenths in 1.

· There are $3\frac{1}{2}$ sevenths in $\frac{1}{2}$ so it's more than that. Actually, it's halfway between $3\frac{1}{2}$ sevenths and 7 sevenths. Maybe about 5 sevenths.

hot **words** | inverse
reciprocal

Homework

page 40

8 Powerhouse Show-Off

ADDING, SUBTRACTING, MULTIPLYING, AND DIVIDING FRACTIONS

What about adding, subtracting, multiplying, and dividing with mixed numbers? After you investigate problems involving mixed numbers, it will be your turn to be the teacher. You will write true and false statements about a set of fraction problems and summarize what you have learned by writing a Number Powerhouse Guide to fraction operations.

Investigate Operations with Mixed Numbers

How can you use what you know about operating with fractions to solve problems involving mixed numbers?

The problems in the box below involve mixed numbers. Use what you know about fraction operations to think about and solve the problems.

1 For each problem in the box, write at least one statement about the answer that you know must be true. Do this without solving the problem.

2 Which of the problems can you solve mentally? Choose at least two problems you think you can solve mentally. For each problem, write the answer and describe your thinking.

3 For the problems that you did not solve mentally, find solutions using pencil and paper. Record your work.

Mixed-Number Problems

a. $1\frac{1}{2} + 1\frac{1}{3}$ b. $3\frac{1}{4} - 1\frac{1}{2}$ c. $2\frac{5}{8} + 3\frac{1}{4}$ d. $4\frac{3}{10} - 3\frac{3}{5}$

e. $2\frac{2}{3} \times 3\frac{1}{2}$ f. $1\frac{3}{4} \div 2\frac{1}{2}$ g. $3\frac{1}{2} \div \frac{1}{4}$ h. $\frac{1}{6} \div 2\frac{1}{3}$

Write True and False Statements

You will come up with true and false statements about fraction problems to be used for a class test. Think about what you know for sure about the answer to each fraction problem.

How can you use what you know about estimating answers to fraction problems to write true and false statements?

1 Choose a pair of fractions from the handout Number Powerhouse Fraction Bank. Use the pair of fractions to write an addition, subtraction, multiplication, and division problem. Be sure to choose a pair of fractions that will be challenging enough for your classmates.

2 Write three statements for each problem. Two of the statements should be true, and one should be false. Use the following words to start your three statements:
   a. The answer is greater than _____.
   b. The answer is less than _____.
   c. The answer is equal to _____.

3 Be prepared to present a problem to the class. Your classmates will try to pick out the false statement.

Write Your Own Number Powerhouse Guide

Think about what you've learned about adding, subtracting, multiplying, and dividing fractions. Write your own Number Powerhouse Guide to operating with fractions using these guidelines.

- Use a set of four problems as your examples.

- Describe ways to think about some of the problems to come up with an answer mentally.

- Describe ways to think about some of the problems to come up with an estimate.

- Show ways to solve some of the problems by following rules and using pencil and paper.

hot**words** | mixed number
improper fraction

page 41

PHASE THREE

In this phase you will be making sense of decimal operations as you think about money and play a game. Figuring out where the decimal point goes when you are adding, subtracting, multipying, and dividing decimals is important. You will become an expert at figuring out the percent of any number, too!

Think about how decimals and percents are used in everyday experience. How can mental math and estimation help you come up with quick answers?

Decimal and Percent Power

WHAT'S THE MATH?

Investigations in this section focus on:

COMPUTATION

- Understanding decimals and percents

- Adding, subtracting, multiplying, and dividing decimals and understanding where the decimal point should be placed

- Using paper and pencil, calculator, and mental math to get exact answers with decimals and percents

ESTIMATION

- Using estimation to determine where the decimal point goes

- Using estimation to check whether or not the results make sense

9 Making Cents of Decimals

When you buy something and get change, how do you know the total was right and that you got the correct change? Thinking about money helps you make sense of adding and subtracting decimals. Then, by estimating and using mental math for adding and subtracting decimals, you can determine where to place the decimal point without a doubt!

Use Decimals to Make Change

How can you use decimal addition and subtraction to calculate change?

When you make change, you have to solve two problems: How much should the customer get back, and what's the best way to give the change? In this investigation, you will solve both of these problems.

1 For each receipt shown, find the amount of change you should give mentally (by doing the math in your head) and write it down.

2 For each receipt, use pencil and paper to solve the problem. Write the entire equation. Check this answer against your estimations.

3 No one wants a pocket full of pennies and nickels! Tell in writing how you would give the change to the customer using the *fewest* possible coins and/or dollar bills for each receipt.

4 Check your answers to item **3** by writing and solving an addition problem in which you add up the change for each receipt.

| apple | $0.50 |
| CASH GIVEN | $0.75 |

| small drink | $0.74 |
| CASH GIVEN | $0.80 |

| laundry detergent | $3.20 |
| CASH GIVEN | $5.00 |

| 15 lbs. dog food | $21.68 |
| CASH GIVEN | $22.00 |

| paperback book | $7.36 |
| CASH GIVEN | $12.41 |

Make Decimal Decisions

The placement of the decimal point can make a big difference, such as the difference between an answer of 140.57 and an answer of 14.057 or 1.4057. In this investigation you will use mental math and estimation skills to determine the placement of the decimal point and to identify errors in decimal addition and subtraction problems.

Without recalculating, how can you tell where the decimal point belongs in an answer, or whether an error was made in the calculation?

1 Copy items **a** through **d** shown below. Use your estimation skills to locate the decimal point in each answer. (You may need to add one or more zeros to the answer.) For each problem, write a short explanation telling how you decided where the decimal point should go.

a. $15 + 25 = 400$

$1.5 + 2.5 = 400$

$0.15 + 0.25 = 400$

b. $0.573 - 0.335 = 238$

$5.73 - 3.35 = 238$

$57.3 - 33.5 = 238$

c. $104.87 + 245.002 = 349872$ **d.** $14.4 - 33.81 = 1941$

2 Each problem below shows a correct solution and an incorrect solution that could result if someone wasn't careful about the decimal point when adding or subtracting. For each problem, use mental arithmetic or estimation to figure out which is the correct solution. Then write about the error someone might have made to arrive at the incorrect solution.

a. For the problem $0.412 + 0.3$, is the correct solution 0.712 or 0.415?

b. For the problem $0.5 - 0.01$, is the correct solution 0.4 or 0.49?

3 Make up two decimal addition problems and two decimal subtraction problems of your own. Use the calculator to find the answer to each problem. Check your answers to see that they are reasonable. Then write about some errors to watch out for when using a calculator to add or subtract decimals.

hot **words** | addition subtraction

Homework

 page 42

10 The Cost Is Correct

INVESTIGATING
DECIMAL
MULTIPLICATION
AND DIVISION

You have learned where the decimal point belongs in problems that involve adding and subtracting. Do you think it would be the same for multiplication and division problems? You will play a game that shows what you know about decimal multiplication and division, and then use your estimation skills to figure out where the decimal point goes.

How can you think out answers to decimal multiplication and division problems?

Play "The Cost Is Correct" Game

Your teacher will give you a handout, Rules for "The Cost Is Correct." The game gives two questions to answer: What's the cost? and What's the weight? This is a mental math game—no calculators today. First you will play some practice rounds. In your practice rounds, check your answers to make sure your strategies are working.

1 Play Practice Rounds 1, 2, and 3, using the information given below to answer the question, "What's the Cost?"

2 Play Practice Rounds 4, 5, and 6, using the information given below to answer the question, "What's the Weight?"

3 After your practice rounds, play the game using the numbers the teacher gives you. This time you will have to figure out which question to answer, as described in the handout Rules for "The Cost Is Correct."

What's the Cost and Weight?

What's the Cost?	What's the Weight?
Practice Round 1: 4 pounds of raisins	Practice Round 4: $2.80
Practice Round 2: 1.5 pounds of raisins	Practice Round 5: $3.50
Practice Round 3: 2.75 pounds of granola	Practice Round 6: $0.75

Locate the Decimal Point

If your calculator tells you that $14.27 \times 2.2 = 313.94$, did you press the right keys? Use the problems in the box below. Follow these steps to try to figure out where the decimal point goes when you multiply and divide decimals.

How can you tell where the decimal point belongs in an answer?

1 Copy the problems in Set 1. Use your estimation skills to locate the decimal point in each answer. (You may need to add one or more zeros to the answer.) Then solve the problems on the calculator to see how close your estimates were.

2 Calculate the answers to the problems shown in Set 2. For each problem, write a short explanation telling how you decided where the decimal point should go. Then check your answers on the calculator.

Write About Decimal Dilemmas

Now it's time to return to Decimal Dilemmas. Use the handout Decimal Dilemmas to explain your strategy for each question. Be ready to share your strategies.

Decimal Problems

Set 1	Set 2
a. $21 \times 11 = 231$	**a.** $6.2 \div 0.8 = \underline{\quad}$
$2.1 \times 11 = 231$	**b.** $74.23 \times 10.877 = \underline{\quad}$
$2.1 \times 1.1 = 231$	**c.** $89.4 \times 105.765 = \underline{\quad}$
b. $870 \div 2.5 = 348$	**d.** $123.42 \div 0.217 = \underline{\quad}$
$870 \div 25 = 348$	
$8.70 \div 2.5 = 348$	
$870 \div 0.25 = 348$	
c. $92 \times 1.5 = 1380$	
$0.92 \times 0.15 = 1380$	
d. $0.6 \div 0.3 = 2000$	
$0.06 \div 0.3 = 2000$	
$0.6 \div 0.03 = 2000$	

hot **words** | multiplication / division

Homework

 page 43

Percent Powerhouse

FINDING A PERCENT OF A NUMBER

Amaze your friends! Impress your parents! By using simple percent values like 50%, 10%, and 1%, you can calculate percents of any number!

How can you mentally find 50%, 10%, and 1% of a number?

Find Important Percents

Three of the most important percent values are 50%, 10%, and 1%. Fortunately, these are percents that you can calculate quickly. As you work with the lists of numbers your class comes up with, you will discover strategies for finding 50%, 10%, and 1% of a number.

1 Work with List A.

  a. Choose one number from List A. On your own, find 50%, 10%, and 1% of that number. Use any strategy that makes sense to you. Write down each answer and explain how you found it.

  b. On your own, find 50%, 10%, and 1% of another number on List A. See if you can use a strategy that is different from the one you used to find percents of the first number. Look for patterns in your answers.

  c. Share your answers and strategies with your partner. Discuss any patterns you see.

  d. With your partner, find 50%, 10%, and 1% of any numbers on List A that you have not worked with. Remember to write down your answers and strategies.

2 Work with List B.

  a. With your partner, choose at least three numbers in List B. Find 50%, 10%, and 1% of each number.

  b. When you have finished, write a short paragraph on your own explaining how you can quickly find 50%, 10%, and 1% of *any* number.

Find 1% to 99% of Any Number

How can you find any percent of a number?

In this investigation, you will use your ability to find 50%, 10%, and 1% of a number to calculate other percents. Use the table in the handout Finding Any Percent and follow these steps with a partner.

1 Across the top row of the table, fill in any six percents. (Do not include 1%, 10%, or 50%.) In the left-hand column, fill in at least six whole numbers from 25 to 2,000. Include two-, three-, and four-digit numbers.

2 Complete the table. When you cannot find an exact answer, give a good estimate. Circle any answers that are not exact. (Do not use a calculator for this part of the investigation.)

3 Exchange your table with another pair of students. Use a calculator to check their answers. Keep track of any errors you find. If an answer is an estimate, think about whether it is "close enough" to the exact answer before you mark it as an error. Meet with the other pair and report any errors that you think you found. Then exchange tables again so that you have your original table.

4 Check any answers in your original table that may be errors. Remember that your original answer may be correct!

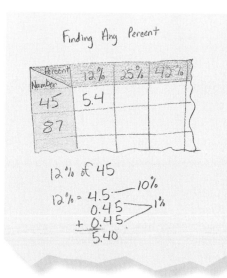

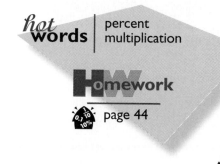

hot words | percent
multiplication

Homework

page 44

Powerhouse Challenge

You have investigated operations with whole numbers, integers, fractions, and decimals, and you have found ways to calculate a percent of a number. Now it's time to use all of the calculation and estimation skills you have learned.

Solve Percent Problems

How can you use percents to solve real-world problems?

Your strategies for finding the percent of a number can help you in real-world situations. For each situation, write down your answer and explain how you found it. If you cannot give an exact answer, make a good estimate.

1 Tips: An average tip for a waiter is 15% of the amount on the bill. Suppose your family's dinner bill comes to $48. How much would a 15% tip be?

2 Sale Price: CD Conspiracy is having a "25% off" sale. If a CD usually costs $12.00, how much would you save? What would the sale price be?

3 **BLOWOUT** Sale Price: CD Conspiracy decides to hold a "45% off" sale! During this sale, how much would you save on a $12.00 CD? What is the sale price?

4 Income tax: In 1996, 28% of Selma's total salary went to federal and state income tax. If she earned $35,128.00, how much income tax did she pay?

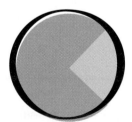

5 Statistics: In 1990, 87% of the population of Utah lived in urban areas (cities and towns). If Utah's 1990 population was 1,461,037, how many people lived in urban areas?

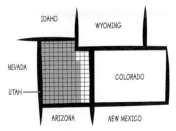

Close In on the Targets

Copy each equation below. Using only the numerals 1 through 6, fill in the boxes to come as close as you can to each target number. Then write how far off you were from the target number. You may use each numeral only *once* in any equation. When you have finished, find your total score. Your score depends on how close you get!

Can you arrange digits in an equation to give an exact answer?

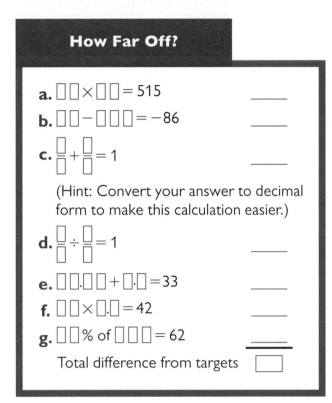

How Far Off?

a. $\square\square \times \square\square = 515$ ____

b. $\square\square - \square\square\square = -86$ ____

c. $\dfrac{\square}{\square} + \dfrac{\square}{\square} = 1$ ____

(Hint: Convert your answer to decimal form to make this calculation easier.)

d. $\dfrac{\square}{\square} \div \dfrac{\square}{\square} = 1$ ____

e. $\square\square.\square\square + \square.\square = 33$ ____

f. $\square\square \times \square.\square = 42$ ____

g. $\square\square\% \text{ of } \square\square\square = 62$ ____

Total difference from targets $\boxed{}$

Write About Operations

A student who is about to begin this unit has some questions for you. So that you don't give away too much, choose only *two* of the student's questions to answer.

- My teacher says that it is important to add, subtract, multiply, and divide in the right order. Is this true? Why does the order matter?

- What are the most important things to know about adding and subtracting signed numbers?

- I've heard that it is hard to add and subtract fractions. Is it? What did you learn that helped you?

- Someone told me that you can find percents in your head. How do you do it?

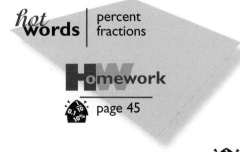

hot **words** | percent fractions

Homework

page 45

Start with What You Know

Applying Skills

For items **1–8**, write an estimate for each problem. Then calculate the answer for each problem and check to see how close your estimate is to the answer.

1. 128 + 54

2. 78 ÷ 3

3. 32 × 18

4. 564 − 208

5. 7,986 + 4,062

6. 6,761 − 4,308

7. 63 × 21

8. 8,964 ÷ 9

For items **9** and **10**, write down which statements are true for each problem without calculating the exact answer.

9. 3,862 ÷ 92

   a. The answer is 44.

   b. The answer is not less than 40.

   c. The answer is greater than 35.

   d. The answer is less than 50.

10. 452 × 162

   a. The answer is greater than 40,000.

   b. The answer is less than 100,000.

   c. The answer is not less than 50,000.

   d. The answer is 53,000.

For items **11–14**, find the exact answer for each problem using two different methods. Remember to show your work. If you use mental math or sketches, record the thinking and any sketches you used.

11. 156 added to 28

12. 47 times 22

13. 96 divided by 4

14. 451 minus 380

Extending Concepts

Use this information for items **15** and **16**: Beatrice is putting new carpet in her 1,692-square-foot apartment. The cost is $23.00 for 3 square feet.

15. Estimate and calculate the cost of putting carpet in the entire apartment.

16. Explain how you estimated the cost. Did your method come close? Why or why not? If it did not, how could you improve your method?

Writing

Use the following to answer item **17**: Benji is planning a vacation to Mali in western Africa to visit the ancient salt center, Timbuktu. The table shows his estimates of expenses for the trip. He thinks he can pay for everything with $3,000.

Cost per Unit	Estimate
One-way airfare at $928	$1,000
Meals @ $5/meal (36 meals)	100
Hotel @ $35/night (12 nights)	600
Jeep rental @ $75/day (12 days)	1,000
Gas @ $30/tank (3 tanks)	100
Spending money	200
TOTAL	$3,000

17. Write a letter to Benji telling whether or not you agree that he can pay for everything with $3,000. Include your results from checking Benji's estimates and your calculations of the exact costs.

Following the Laws of Order

Applying Skills

Use the order of operations on page 9 to evaluate the expressions in items **1–14**.

1. $(9 \div 3) \times 2^3 - (1 + 2)$

2. $(14 \div 2) + 3^2 \times (6 - 2)$

3. $3 + 6 - 2^2 \times (16 \div 8)$

4. $14 - (3 \times 2) \div 2 + 1$

5. $12 + 4^3 \div 2 \times 3$

6. $(12 + 4) \times (18 \div 3) + 2$

7. $(4,572 - 2,381) \times 2^8 - 681$

8. $3^9 - 6,072 + 43$

9. $64 \times (5^4 \div 5)$

10. $4 + 1,622 \times 12 + 178$

11. $179 + (6^4 \div 2) \div 6$

12. Eight times five plus twelve divided by three.

13. Sixteen divided by two plus sixty minus forty-two.

14. Forty-seven plus six divided by three plus four.

Extending Concepts

15. Explain why 30 divided by 5 can also be written as $\frac{30}{5}$. Illustrate your answer by drawing a picture of 30 divided by 5 and $\frac{30}{5}$.

16. Think about the order of operations. Give reasons why mathematicians have agreed to use this specific order. If you agree with this order, explain why it makes sense to you. If you believe another order would make more sense, write your revised order of operations and give reasons why this new method makes sense. Be sure to include pictures and/or examples.

For items **17–20**, put operations and grouping symbols into each number list to write an expression that results in the smallest whole number possible.

17. 5, 2, 4, 9, 1

18. 8, 6, 1, 7, 2

19. 3, 5, 7, 9, 2

20. 2, 4, 6, 8, 7

For items **21–24**, put operations and grouping symbols into each number list to write as many different expressions as you can that result in whole numbers.

21. 2, 3, 4, 5, 6

22. 8, 9, 5, 4, 3

23. 3, 5, 6, 2, 1

24. 7, 5, 6, 8, 9

Writing

25. Answer the letter to Dr. Math.

Dear Dr. Math,

I'm confused! I think that twenty-five divided by five plus two times five equals thirty-five, but my friend Cedric says it's fifteen. Now he's talking about expressions and parentheses. What is he talking about, and who is right?

Confused Connie

Know How to Read the Signs

Applying Skills

For items **1–4**, look at the cubes shown. If pink is positive and green is negative, write a problem that the cubes show. Describe how you would solve the problem.

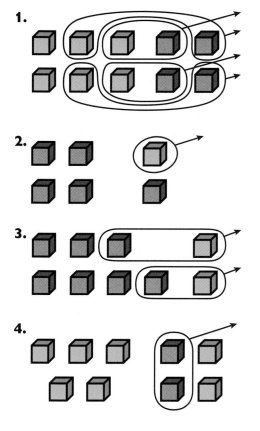

1.

2.

3.

4.

For items **5–12**, solve each problem.

5. $3 + 6$ **6.** $3 + (-6)$

7. $(-9) + 6$ **8.** $6 - (-3)$

9. $4 - (-2)$ **10.** $(-8) - (-4)$

11. $5 + 2$ **12.** $10 + (-8)$

Extending Concepts

13. Explain the difference between positive and negative numbers.

For items **14 and 15**, use the following:
My friend Judy loves shopping at the mall. She spends an increasing amount of money each week. Three weeks ago she spent $3, two weeks ago she spent $9, and last week she spent $27. She charges everything, so she is going further into debt each time she shops.

14. Write an equation that shows how much money Judy has spent so far. Explain your thinking.

15. Today Judy decided to take a $25 sweater back to the store. Explain how this affects her debt situation.

Making Connections

Use the following information for item **16:**
The temperature on Monday was 40 degrees Fahrenheit. On Tuesday, the temperature went down 15 degrees. On Wednesday, the temperature fell another 35 degrees. Thursday, the temperature rose 8 degrees. Finally on Friday, the temperature increased by 16 degrees.

16. What was the temperature at the end of the week? You may want to draw a picture to show your answer.

The Problems Are All Yours

Applying Skills

1. Which of the following expressions equal 1? Explain why or why not.

   a. $3 - 2$ **b.** $1 - (-1)$

   c. $1 + 1$ **d.** $2 - (-1)$

2. Which of the following expressions equal 7? Explain why or why not.

   a. $3 + 4$ **b.** $(-2) + (-5)$

   c. $(-3) + 10$ **d.** $(-10) + 3$

3. Which of the following expressions equal 12? Explain why or why not.

   a. $(-17) + 5$ **b.** $(-8) + 20$

   c. $9 + 3$ **d.** $(-13) + 25$

For items **4–11**, write a list of at least three equations that will work for the answers given. Include addition and subtraction equations, and positive and negative numbers.

   4. 2 **5.** 3 **6.** 4

   7. 5 **8.** 11 **9.** 14

   10. 56 **11.** 37

Extending Concepts

12. Write one integer subtraction problem and calculate the answer for it. Give step-by-step instructions for solving the problem.

13. Write one problem that involves estimation and calculate the answer for it. Give step-by-step instructions for solving the problem.

14. Write one problem for which someone would have to use the order of operations. (Be sure to include parentheses, powers, addition, subtraction, multiplication, and division.) Calculate the answer for it. Give step-by-step instructions for solving the problem.

Writing

15. Answer the letter to Dr. Math.

> Dear Dr. Math,
>
> I know how to add two numbers when there are positive and negative signs, but what about adding three or more numbers? My older sister said $(-1) + 5 + 4 = 8$, but she couldn't tell me why. I'd like to know why. Can you explain this?
>
> Expressionless

Pluses and Minuses

Applying Skills

For items **1–4,** answer this question: If you combined the shaded portions of the two circles, what fraction of a circle would you have?

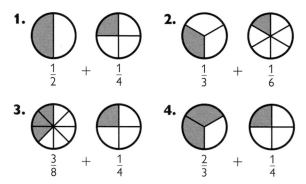

1. $\frac{1}{2}$ + $\frac{1}{4}$

2. $\frac{1}{3}$ + $\frac{1}{6}$

3. $\frac{3}{8}$ + $\frac{1}{4}$

4. $\frac{2}{3}$ + $\frac{1}{4}$

For items **5–8,** solve the addition problems mentally. Use sketches or words to help.

5. $\frac{1}{2} + \frac{2}{3}$

6. $\frac{4}{6} + \frac{3}{5}$

7. $\frac{1}{5} + \frac{1}{10}$

8. $\frac{1}{6} + \frac{7}{8}$

For items **9–12,** solve the subtraction problems mentally. Use sketches or words to help.

9. $\frac{5}{8} - \frac{1}{3}$

10. $\frac{3}{5} - \frac{1}{10}$

11. $\frac{1}{6} - \frac{1}{9}$

12. $\frac{2}{5} - \frac{1}{10}$

For items **13–16,** solve the problems mentally, or use paper and pencil.

13. $\frac{1}{2} - \frac{1}{4}$

14. $\frac{1}{12} + \frac{5}{6}$

15. $\frac{3}{10} + \frac{1}{2}$

16. $\frac{7}{15} - \frac{4}{15}$

Extending Concepts

17. Andrew is measuring the perimeter of a very small object. He found that it measured $\frac{1}{2}''$ on two sides and $\frac{1}{3}''$ on the other two sides. What is the perimeter of the object? Show how you solved the problem. What do you think the object might be?

18. Find two fractions whose sum is $\frac{5}{12}$ and whose difference is $\frac{1}{4}$. Explain how you figured it out.

Making Connections

For items **19–22,** use the information shown about musical notes. Draw one note that is equal to the sum of the notes in each item.

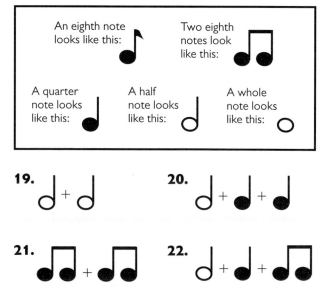

Notes in Music

An eighth note looks like this:

Two eighth notes look like this:

A quarter note looks like this:

A half note looks like this:

A whole note looks like this:

19.

20.

21.

22.

Multiplication Made Easy

Applying Skills

For the problems in items **1–6**, use words to write the multiplication question. Then find the exact answer using mental math. You may use sketches and words to help.

1. $\frac{1}{3} \times \frac{1}{6}$ **2.** $\frac{1}{6} \times \frac{7}{8}$ **3.** $\frac{1}{2} \times \frac{3}{8}$

4. $4 \times \frac{3}{4}$ **5.** $\frac{1}{4} \times \frac{1}{6}$ **6.** $\frac{1}{3} \times \frac{2}{3}$

For items **7–9**, estimate the answer for each problem and write about what you can say for sure.

7. $\frac{1}{4} \times \frac{9}{10}$ **8.** $\frac{2}{3} \times \frac{16}{17}$ **9.** $\frac{3}{4} \times \frac{6}{11}$

For items **10–12**, solve the problems by following the rules for multiplying fractions that you reviewed in class.

10. $\frac{2}{7} \times \frac{3}{5}$ **11.** $\frac{1}{12} \times \frac{9}{10}$ **12.** $\frac{4}{5} \times \frac{7}{15}$

13. Vince says he spends $\frac{1}{3}$ of his 24-hour day sleeping and another $\frac{1}{4}$ of his day in school. How much time does he have for other activities? Explain your answer.

Extending Concepts

15. Wendy's uncle has decided to help her pay for her guitar lessons for the next three years. The lessons cost $850 per year. Plans A–C show how much Wendy's uncle would pay. Choose the plan that is the best deal for Wendy. Explain your thinking.

Plan A: Year 1: $\frac{3}{5}$ of the tuition
Year 2: $\frac{11}{20}$ of the tuition
Year 3: $\frac{6}{15}$ of the tuition

Plan B: Year 1: all of the tuition
Year 2: $\frac{7}{10}$ of the tuition
Year 3: none of the tuition

Plan C: $\frac{8}{25}$ of the total tuition for all three years

Making Connections

Use the following for items **15–17:**
The table below shows the top ten favorite words to use and the probability of each word appearing in a Valentine. The probability for the word *cute* is $\frac{3}{11}$. Suppose you are sending 25 Valentines. Since $25 \times \frac{3}{11}$ is $\frac{75}{11}$, or $6\frac{9}{11}$, *cute* is likely to appear about 7 times among the cards you are sending.

15. How many times might the word *athletic* appear?

16. How many times might the word *happy* appear?

17. Choose a different word from the table. How many times might that word appear?

Valentine Trivia

Word	Probability
funny	$\frac{3}{7}$
smart	$\frac{7}{18}$
kind	$\frac{11}{27}$
cute	$\frac{3}{11}$
happy	$\frac{2}{5}$
friendly	$\frac{5}{12}$
loyal	$\frac{3}{10}$
pretty	$\frac{2}{9}$
athletic	$\frac{1}{6}$
interesting	$\frac{2}{7}$

The Great Fraction Divide

Applying Skills

For the problems in items **1–6**, use words to write the division question. Then find the exact answer using mental math. You may use sketches and words to help.

1. $\dfrac{1}{8} \div \dfrac{1}{4}$ **2.** $\dfrac{1}{3} \div \dfrac{1}{2}$ **3.** $\dfrac{1}{6} \div \dfrac{2}{3}$

4. $\dfrac{1}{3} \div \dfrac{3}{4}$ **5.** $\dfrac{7}{8} \div \dfrac{2}{3}$ **6.** $\dfrac{7}{9} \div \dfrac{1}{5}$

For items **7–12**, estimate the answer for each problem and write about what you can say for sure.

7. $\dfrac{2}{3} \div \dfrac{11}{12}$ **8.** $\dfrac{1}{9} \div \dfrac{5}{6}$ **9.** $\dfrac{7}{8} \div \dfrac{2}{15}$

10. $\dfrac{7}{12} \div \dfrac{5}{8}$ **11.** $\dfrac{13}{15} \div \dfrac{4}{9}$ **12.** $\dfrac{3}{14} \div \dfrac{3}{24}$

For items **13–18**, solve the problems by following the rules for dividing fractions that you reviewed in class discussion.

13. $\dfrac{2}{3} \div \dfrac{1}{4}$ **14.** $\dfrac{3}{8} \div \dfrac{2}{9}$ **15.** $\dfrac{5}{6} \div \dfrac{3}{4}$

16. $\dfrac{12}{16} \div \dfrac{2}{5}$ **17.** $\dfrac{15}{16} \div \dfrac{4}{5}$ **18.** $\dfrac{4}{5} \div \dfrac{3}{4}$

19. An inch is $\frac{1}{12}$ of a foot long. How many inches are there in $\frac{5}{6}$ of a foot? Show your thinking.

20. Rachel has a science project to do. She figures she can get $\frac{1}{4}$ of it done in $\frac{3}{4}$ of an hour. How long will it take her to complete the project? Explain your answer.

Extending Concepts

For items **21–22**, use the order of operations to solve the problems.

21. $\left(\dfrac{1}{8} + \dfrac{1}{4} \right) \div \dfrac{2}{3}$

22. $\left(\dfrac{1}{8} + \dfrac{3}{4} \right) \div \left(\dfrac{2}{3} - \dfrac{1}{6} \right)$

23. Joshua is confused about how to divide fractions. Write a set of rules for dividing fractions that he can follow. Be sure to explain why each step works and include sample problems.

Making Connections

24. On a recent dig near Brea, California, the archeologist X. K. Vator unearthed a mysterious clay tablet with strange symbols. The English translation is shown below. To celebrate this discovery, Dr. Vator asks her chef to make Woolly Mammoth Stew for 18 people. Use fraction division equations to figure out how much of each ingredient the chef will need.

Woolly Mammoth Stew (Serves 8)
3 Pleistocine onions, chopped
28 lbs Woolly Mammoth meat, cubed
8 edible tubers, sliced
$\frac{1}{2}$ cup hot tar or molasses
$\frac{2}{3}$ tbsp salt

Powerhouse Show-Off

Applying Skills

For items **1–6**, solve the problems mentally, or use paper and pencil.

1. $1\frac{1}{2} - \frac{2}{3}$ **2.** $3\frac{4}{5} \times 1\frac{5}{6}$ **3.** $1\frac{2}{7} \times 1\frac{3}{5}$

4. $\frac{1}{3} + 2\frac{8}{9}$ **5.** $1\frac{6}{7} - 1\frac{4}{5}$ **6.** $3\frac{2}{3} \div \frac{6}{9}$

7. Choose four of the problems in items **1–6.** Write three statements for each problem. Two of the statements should be true. One of the statements should be false. Circle the one that is false.

For items **8 and 9**, write an equation to solve the problem. Write a sentence explaining why the equation solves the problem.

8. Keisha and eleven prospecting partners were looking for gold. They discovered $\frac{5}{6}$ pound of gold. If each partner received $\frac{1}{12}$ of the gold, how much did each one get?

9. Keisha then found another $\frac{1}{12}$ of a pound. How much gold was discovered altogether?

Extending Concepts

For items **10–15**, decide which of the statements should be rules. A rule is a statement that is always true. If you believe that a statement is a rule, write a short explanation telling why it works. If a statement is not a rule, show a counterexample. A counterexample is an example that makes the statement false.

Hint: An easy way to begin testing a statement is to think of an example and see if it works. For item **10**, you could start by testing whether or not $\frac{1}{3} + \frac{1}{2} = \frac{2}{5}$.

10. When you add two fractions, the numerator of the answer is the sum of their numerators, and the denominator of the answer is the sum of their denominators.

11. To subtract fractions with different denominators, first write them with the same denominator.

12. You can only add two fractions when one of the denominators divides evenly into the other.

13. You can always find a common denominator for two fractions by multiplying their original denominators.

14. When you subtract fractions with the same numerator, keep the numerator the same and subtract the denominators.

15. To add fractions with different denominators, first write them with the same denominator.

Writing

16. Write a letter to a fifth-grade student explaining how to add, subtract, multiply, and divide fractions. Include example problems and drawings where appropriate.

Making Cents of Decimals

Applying Skills

For items **1** and **2**, copy the equation and put the decimal point in the correct place.

1. $0.007 + 23.6 = 23607$

2. $34.079 - 13.24 = 20839$

For items **3–6**, copy and solve the equation.

3. $1.25 + $0.68 **4.** $13.82 - $6.91

5. $15.3 + 0.062$ **6.** $16.923 + 2.3$

7. Which is greater, 0.3 or 0.08? Why?

8. Asako and her family are planning a camping trip with a budget of $500.00. They would like to buy these items: sleeping bag ($108.35), gas stove ($31.78), tent ($359.20), cook set ($39.42), first-aid kit ($21.89), Global Positioning System ($199.99), compass ($26.14), binoculars ($109.76), knife ($19.56), and lantern ($20.88). What different combinations of camping equipment could Asako's family afford with the money they have? Name as many as you can. Show your work.

Extending Concepts

9. When Miguel adds numbers in his head, he likes to use expanded notation. For example, $1.32 + 0.276$ can be interpreted as $1 + 0 = 1$, and $0.3 + 0.2 = 0.5$, and $0.02 + 0.07 = 0.09$, and $0.000 + 0.006 = 0.006$. The total is added up to make 1.596. Explain what Miguel has done and why it works.

For items **10** and **11,** tell what the next two numbers are in each sequence. Explain how you found out.

10. 10, 10.4, 10.8, 11.2, 11.6, 12.0, …

11. 2, 1.25, 0.5, −0.25, −1, −1.75, …

Making Connections

For items **12–14,** use the following information from *The World Almanac* about platform diving at the Olympic Games.

Year	Name/Country	Points
1948	Victoria M. Draves/U.S.	68.87
1952	Patricia McCormick/U.S.	79.37
1956	Patricia McCormick/U.S.	84.85
1960	Ingrid Kramer/Germany	91.28
1964	Lesley Bush/U.S.	99.80
1968	Milena Duchkova/Czechoslovakia	109.59
1972	Ulrika Knape/Sweden	390.00
1976	Elena Vaytsekhouskaya/USSR	406.59

12. Which two consecutive Olympic years had the greatest difference in points scored? What was the difference?

13. What is the total number of points scored by a diver from the United States in these years?

14. What is the difference between points scored in 1948 and 1976?

The Cost Is Correct

Applying Skills

For items **1–4**, copy the equation and put the decimal point in the correct place.

1. $18.15 \div 5.5 = 33$

2. $38.2 \times 0.032 = 12224$

3. $16.8 \div 0.8 = 21$

4. $6.2 \times 0.876 = 54312$

For items **5–10**, write and solve the equation.

5. 3.722×0.68 **6.** $\$15.61 \times 3$

7. $\$15.50 \div \$0.25$ **8.** $82.26 \div 0.004$

9. $\$27.32 \div 4$ **10.** $\$4.56 \times 5$

11. Choose one multiplication equation and one division equation from items **5–10**. Explain how you decided where the decimal point should be placed in the answer.

12. Vladik's dad filled up the gas tank in his car. The gasoline cost $1.47 per gallon. The total cost of the gasoline was $23.48. Estimate how many gallons of gasoline Vladik's dad put in the tank. Show your thinking.

13. Miwa and her mom went grocery shopping. Her mom bought 2 dozen oranges for $2.69 per dozen. Estimate the cost of each orange. Explain how you got your estimate.

14. Alex and Sanjeevi are buying their first home. During the first year, they figure their total mortgage payments will be $12,159.36. How much will their monthly mortage payment be? Show your work.

Extending Concepts

15. Lex wants to invite as many friends as he can to go to the movies with him. He has $20.00. The cost of each ticket is $4.50. Estimate how many friends he can take. A bag of popcorn costs $1.75. Estimate how many friends he can take if he is going to buy everyone, including himself, a bag of popcorn.

For items **16–18**, give the next two numbers in each sequence. Explain how you found out. You might want to use a calculator.

16. 5, 6.5, 8.45, 10.985, 14.2805, 18.56465, …

17. 15.8, 31.6, 63.2, 126.4, 252.8, 505.6, …

18. 4, 10, 25, 62.5, 156.25, 390.625, …

19. Write an addition or subtraction sequence of your own. Include at least six numbers.

20. Write a multiplication sequence of your own. Include at least six numbers.

Writing

21. Answer the letter to Dr. Math.

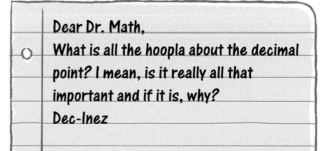

Dear Dr. Math,
What is all the hoopla about the decimal point? I mean, is it really all that important and if it is, why?
Dec-Inez

Percent Powerhouse

Applying Skills

For items **1–6**, find 50%, 10%, and 1% of each number. Write your strategies.

1. 58   **2.** 116   **3.** 293

4. 41   **5.** 1,080   **6.** 1,593

For items **7–13**, find the percent of each number without using a calculator. Circle the answers that are estimates.

7. 32% of 68   **8.** 7% of 92

9. 66% of 43   **10.** 100% of 1,062

11. 62.5% of 51   **12.** 1.3% of 100

13. 156% of 22

14. Choose two problems that you solved in items **7–13**. Explain how you solved each one.

For items **15–18**, change the percents to decimals.

15. 62%   **16.** 83%   **17.** 4%   **18.** 157%

Extending Concepts

19. Ask five people which of the following colors is their favorite: blue, green, red, or yellow. Show the results in percents. Make a graph to illustrate your findings.

20. Now ask ten people a question of your own. Be sure to ask a question that has between two and five possible answers. Do not use a question that has a yes/no answer. Show your findings with percents and a graph.

21. One day a gardener picked about 20% of all the strawberries in his garden. Later that day, his wife picked about 25% of the remaining strawberries. Still later, the son of the gardener picked about 33% of the strawberries that were left. Even later, the daughter picked about 50% of the remaining strawberries in the garden. Finally, there were only 3 strawberries left. About how many strawberries were originally in the garden? Explain.

Making Connections

For a healthy diet, the total calories a person consumes should be no more than 30% fat. Tell whether the foods in items **22–25** meet these recommendations. Show how you found your answer.

22. "Reduced-fat" chips
Calories per serving: 140
Calories from fat: 70

23. "Low-fat" snack bar
Calories per serving: 150
Calories from fat: 25

24. "Light" popcorn
Calories per serving: 20
Calories from fat: 5

25. "Healthy" soup
Calories per serving: 110
Calories from fat: 25

Powerhouse Challenge

Applying Skills

For items **1–11**, solve and show your work. Round your answer to the nearest hundredth.

1. Find 8.5% of $32.16.

2. Find 15% of $87.17.

3. Find 25% of 1,061.

4. Find 2.5% of 587.

5. Find the total cost of a $25.50 meal after a tax of 8.5% and a tip of 15% is added.

6. A shirt that sold for $49.99 has been marked down 30%. Find the sale price.

7. In 1996, 27% of Camille's income went to state and federal taxes. If she earned $35,672.00, how much did she actually keep?

8. Jared's uncle bought 100 shares of stock for $37.25 a share. In 6 months the stock went up 30%. How much were the 100 shares of stock worth in 6 months?

9. Emily went to the doctor for an annual physical. The nurse measured her height and weight. She said that Emily's height had increased by 10% and her weight had increased by 5% since her physical last year. Emily weighs 95 pounds and is 5 feet tall this year. What were her height and weight at last year's physical?

10. Kyal's family bought a treadmill on sale. It was 25% off the original price of $1,399.95. They paid $\frac{1}{2}$ of the sales price as a down payment. What was the down payment?

11. Zachary and his family went on a vacation to San Francisco last summer. On the first day, they gave the taxi driver a 15% tip and the hotel bell boy $2.00 for taking the luggage to the room. The taxi fare was $15.75. How much did they spend in all?

Extending Concepts

12. Explain the connection between fractions, decimals, and percents. Show examples to illustrate your thinking.

13. Which concept is easier for you to understand—fractions, decimals, or percents? Why?

14. Describe a real-world problem or situation in which you would use fractions, decimals, or percents. Tell how you would solve the problem.

15. Make at least four equations similar to the one shown. Make sure you have fractions, decimals, and percents in your equations. Ask someone in your family to try to get as close as they can to the target number by filling in the boxes, using only the numerals 1 through 6.

$\square\square \times \square . \square = 42$ How far off?

Writing

16. What is the most important concept you have learned in *Number Powerhouse*? Tell how the concept works and why it is important.

STUDENT GALLERY

CREDITS: Photography: Chris Conroy • Beverley Harper (cover) •
© SuperStock: pp. 2, 3TM, 7, 14, 20, 28, 33 • © Petrified Collection/
The Image Bank: pp. 11B, 27. Illustrations: © Rob Blackard: pp. 26, 32, 40.

Creative Publications and MathScape are trademarks or registered
trademarks of Creative Publications.

© 1998 Creative Publications

Two Prudential Plaza, Suite 1175
Chicago, IL 60601

Printed in the United States of America.

0-7622-0211-4

4 5 6 7 8 9 10 . 02 01 00